WHY THE CROSS?

John Blanchard

 BOOKS

EP Books, Faverdale North, Darlington, DL3 0PH, England
e-mail: sales@epbooks.org
web: www.epbooks.org

EP Books USA, P. O. Box 614, Carlisle, PA 17013, USA
e-mail: usasales@epbooks.org
web: www.epbooks.us

First published 2011

British Library Cataloguing in Publication Data available

ISBN-13 978 085234 738 6   ISBN 0 85234 738 3

Printed and bound in the UK by **hpm** group, www.hpm.uk.com

WHY THE CROSS?

On the morning of 28 January 1970 two friends and I drove cautiously towards Checkpoint Charlie, the best-known crossing point in the

Checkpoint Charlie

Berlin Wall, part of the infamous Iron Curtain that divided Communist Eastern Europe from the free West after the end of World War II. An armed guard examined our personal papers, then asked for the documents relating to the car. I suddenly realized that we might now be in trouble. The Volks- wagen's registration book was in the name of the Movement for World Evangelization, of which my colleagues and I were staff members — an organization that would hardly be welcomed with open arms by a regime that had persecuted the Christian faith for years! With my mind racing, I left the registration book in the glove compartment of the car and handed the guard a wad of impressive-looking literature issued by Volkswagen. Amazingly, he glanced at this and waved us into Eastern Germany.

Like three schoolboys allowed to go home early, we got out of Berlin as fast as we could and headed for Warsaw, just over 300 miles to the east. Heavy snow soon slowed our progress and it was several hours before we reached the Polish border — and faced another crisis. We parked at the remote border post and presented our personal papers. These were accepted, but we were then told to empty the car and bring its entire contents in for examination. Our hearts sank, because of one particular item.

Our original destination had been Czechoslovakia, but another Christian organization had asked whether we would deliver 'some tapes' to Warsaw. Without looking at a map we agreed, thinking that this would not be much of a diversion. We were wrong — by several hundred miles. Our second mistake was to think in terms of a few small cassettes, which we could easily have hidden away. Instead, we were given a large box of fifty reel-to-reel tapes. With no way to hide them, we had simply left the open box on the back seat. This now joined the car's other contents on the counter. 'What are these?', we were asked. Choosing our words carefully we replied, 'A gift from the church in England to the church in Poland.' 'This is too much', the guard enig-matically replied, before disappearing into another room. Moments later he returned and in perfect English ordered, 'Get this out of here before the boss gets back.'

Moments later our precious cargo was safely in Poland. Arriving in Warsaw, we checked into a nondescript hotel which was so cold that we kept our thermal underwear on all night. On the following morning our first task was to get the tapes to their intended destination, so we began scouring the streets trying to find Warsaw's United Evangelical Church. Afraid of speaking to someone hostile to Christianity, we dared not ask directions, but after less than an hour of criss-crossing the city we found it. The building was similar to the many surrounding piles of dreary East European architecture, but something caught our attention and convinced us that we had found the right place. It was a symbol made up of two simple lines, one vertical and the other lying horizontally across it about two-thirds of the way up.

THE SYMBOL

For centuries symbols have been used as a means of identification, often in an immediate, compact and powerful way. Sometimes political or religious extremists do so to claim power or supremacy, to produce fear or insecurity, or even to convey hate or anger. Many are easily recognized, one of the most powerful and emotive being the Nazi swastika. Opponents during the notorious 'Troubles' in Northern Ireland, which lasted for thirty years from the nineteen-sixties and cost over 3,000 lives, often used eye-catching and dramatic symbols. Some of these showed armed and hooded men and covered the outer walls of buildings in Belfast and elsewhere. Strangely, the one that identified our destination in Warsaw represented a barbaric instrument of execution.

Over the centuries, authorities have used many different means of executing criminals and enemies. These have included stoning, the guillotine, the firing squad, hanging, electrocution, gassing and lethal injection. In almost all these cases the death of the victim is instantaneous, while in the others the death throes last only a few minutes. From the fourth century BC onwards at least four powers, including the

Roman Empire, employed a form of execution that was indescribably painful and prolonged — crucifixion. The word comes from the Latin for 'fix to a cross', and this cruel and savage practice was used for about 1,000 years. In AD 337 it was abolished in the Roman Empire by Emperor Constantine I, yet for nearly 2,000 years a cross has been the universally recognized symbol of Christianity, whose founder, Jesus Christ, was crucified on the outskirts of Jerusalem. The British author Malcolm Muggeridge

called it 'the most famous death in history',[1] but what is not immediately obvious is why a cross should be the Christian church's symbol of
choice. It might be difficult to think of one that would represent Jesus'
moral example, or the miracles attributed to him, but at first glance it
seems grotesque to highlight his death in this way.

The symbol of the cross has now been sanitized in such a way that it
seems to have lost its macabre associations. It is on millions of books,
buildings and bodies; it decorates the clothing of countless people
during their lives and is often etched on their gravestones when they
die. There are people for whom the symbol of the cross has a deeply
personal and infinitely precious significance, but for others it is little
more than a charm or good-luck mascot. It is strange that it has such
widespread appeal to millions who have little or no interest in the event
that triggered the trend. Are any other instruments of death universally
popular in these ways? To understand the significance of the cross as a
symbol we need to take a close look at the original event.

THE LAST DAY

Jesus' execution was a judicial death penalty carried out by the Romans,
who occupied Israel at the time. Jesus led a low-profile life in his teens
and twenties, but suddenly came to people's attention when he began
his public teaching at about thirty years of age. Many of the events from
then on were recorded by some of his followers — Matthew, Mark,
Luke and John — each of whom wrote a New Testament book, collec-
tively called 'the Gospels' ('gospel' means 'good news'). Such was the
impact of Jesus' ministry that 'his fame spread throughout all Syria' and
'great crowds followed him from Galilee and the Decapolis, and from
Jerusalem and Judea, and from beyond the Jordan' (Matthew 4:24-25).
Yet not everybody appreciated what he was saying. His teaching
infuriated the religious establishment, especially the Pharisees and the
Sadducees. They had a vested interest in preserving the status quo, and

Jesus' teaching cut across their carefully crafted traditions. The more popular Jesus became, the more they opposed him.

One line of attack was to feed him questions they thought would embarrass or confuse him, but he easily dealt with these, and people were amazed at the way he turned the tables on his enemies (see Matthew 22:23-33). Eventually, his critics decided that there was only one way to stop him: 'The chief priests and the elders of the people ... plotted together in order to arrest Jesus by stealth and kill him' (Matthew 26:3-4). Stealth was needed because they were afraid that the crowds who had seen his miracles would turn against them.

As the situation became increasingly tense, the plotters received help from an unexpected source. Judas Iscariot was the only non-Galilean among Jesus' first disciples, but made such a good impression on the others that they let him handle their corporate funds. This was a bad move because at heart Judas 'was a thief, and having charge of the money bag he used to help himself to what was put into it' (John 12:6). Worse was to follow. Perhaps disappointed that Jesus was not planning to overthrow the Romans, Judas decided to betray him to the religious authorities. They offered him 'thirty pieces of silver' (Matthew 26:15) to do this, and he shook hands on the deal.

Shortly afterwards, Judas identified Jesus to an armed mob by greeting him with a kiss. Jesus was arrested, bound and taken to Annas, who had been the first high priest of the Roman province of Judea. Deposed for exceeding his authority, but still a powerful influence in the land, he 'questioned Jesus about his disciples and his teaching' (John 18:19). When Jesus said that he had always spoken openly, and that if Annas wanted to know what his teaching was he could ask anyone who heard him, one of the officers slapped him in the face and said, 'Is that how you answer the high priest?' (John 18:22). Annas was clearly getting nowhere, so he sent Jesus to his son-in-law Caiaphas, who had been appointed high priest in his place.

The religious authorities were unable to produce any evidence to sustain a charge against Jesus, but two false witnesses testified that he had claimed he would destroy Jerusalem's magnificent temple and rebuild it in three days (see Matthew 26:60-61). Asked by Caiaphas whether this was true, Jesus remained silent. When an infuriated Caiaphas asked him, 'I charge you under oath by the living God: Tell us if you are the Christ, the Son of God', Jesus' reply was electrifying: 'Yes, it is as you say' (Matthew 26:63,64, NIV). This was the last straw for Caiaphas. He declared Jesus guilty of blasphemy, and when he asked the other religious leaders what should be done with him they replied, 'He deserves death' (Matthew 26:66).

Early the next morning the chief priests and elders confirmed the sentence, but as they had no authority to carry it out they took Jesus to Pontius Pilate, the Roman governor of Judea. In the meantime, Judas was suddenly 'seized with remorse' (Matthew 27:3, NIV) and tried to return the thirty pieces of silver, telling the chief priests and elders, 'I have sinned by betraying innocent blood' (Matthew 27:4). When they refused to take the money back, Judas threw the coins into the temple and 'went and hanged himself' (Matthew 27:5).

Standing before Pilate, Jesus refused to respond to the charges brought against him. Frustrated that he could find no fault in Jesus, Pilate suddenly saw a way of offloading the case. When he discovered that Jesus was from Galilee, he sent him to face Herod Antipas, the Jewish ruler of Galilee, who was in Jerusalem at the time.

Herod was glad to handle the case as he had heard a lot about Jesus and even hoped he might see him perform a miracle. He was to be doubly disappointed; not only did Jesus refuse to oblige, he never even opened his mouth, even when Herod 'questioned him at some length' (Luke 23:9). Furious and frustrated, Herod and his soldiers 'treated him with contempt and mocked him' (Luke 23:11) and he was sent back to Pilate.

Pointing out that neither he nor Herod found Jesus guilty of the charges brought against him, Pilate intended scourging Jesus and letting him go, but then thought of a better option. During the annual Passover Feast, an important Jewish festival being celebrated at the time, it was the governor's custom to release one prisoner chosen by the people. Pilate asked the crowd to choose between Jesus and a prisoner called Barabbas, a notorious anarchist and robber. As none of the charges against Jesus could be made to stick, the right choice seemed obvious but, urged on by the religious leaders, the crowd chose

Ruins of the palace of Pontius Pilate

Barabbas. When Pilate asked what should be done with Jesus they shouted, 'Let him be crucified!' Baffled and confused, Pilate asked them, 'Why, what evil has he done?' Ignoring the question, the crowd shouted even louder, 'Let him be crucified!' (Matthew 27:22-23).

Sensing that there could soon be a riot, Pilate told the crowd, 'I am innocent of this man's blood; see to it yourselves' (Matthew 27:24), then washed his hands in a bowl of water as a sign that he was not responsible for what might be about to happen. He then released Barabbas and handed Jesus over to soldiers to be crucified, but with instructions that he should first be scourged. Scourging was a vicious form of torture in which a whip of leather strands loaded with pieces of bone or metal was used to flay the victim, sometimes killing him in the process.

Matthew records what happened next:

> And they stripped him and put a scarlet robe on him, and twisting together a crown of thorns, they put it on his head and put a reed in his right hand. And kneeling before him, they  mocked him, saying, 'Hail, King of the Jews!' And they spat on him and took the reed and struck him on the head. And when they had mocked him, they stripped him of the robe and put his own clothes on him and led him away to crucify him (Matthew 27:28-31).

In crucifixion, the victim was stripped naked and forced to lie face upwards with his shoulders resting on a beam of wood. His outstretched arms were pinned to the beam with nails, possibly driven in just above the wrist. The beam was then lifted up and secured to a large upright post already driven into the ground. Some ancient records point to another nail, or nails, pinning the victim's feet to the upright, and others to a small saddle that would partially support the weight of the body. These were not intended to help the victim, but to keep him alive for longer and so prolong the pain. Some victims suffered appalling agony for several days before dying of blood loss, suffocation, exhaustion, asphyxiation, heart failure, shock, sepsis or dehydration. Unless friends of the deceased claimed the corpse, it was left to the mercy of scavenging birds, stray animals and vermin.

THE FINAL HOURS

Jesus was subjected to humiliating mockery as he hung on the cross, which he accepted without protest or retaliation. The Gospels record him speaking seven times during the crucifixion, and we can note some of them here. The first was to ask God's forgiveness of those responsible for his torture and execution: 'Father, forgive them, for they do not know what they are doing' (Luke 23:34, NIV). He also commended his mother, Mary, to the care of his faithful friend the apostle John, who was standing beside her (see John 19:26-27).

As the end drew near Jesus cried, 'I am thirsty' (John 19:28, NIV). A soldier dipped a sponge into a jar of sour wine, put it on a hyssop branch and held it to his mouth (see John 19:29), a gesture that would have done virtually nothing to quench his raging dehydration. Soon afterwards, Jesus said, 'Father, into your hands I commit my spirit!', then 'breathed his last' (Luke 23:46).

In earlier times it was common in certain cultures to hoist the corpse of an executed criminal on a pole or tree as a final mark of shame. However, Old Testament ceremonial law ruled that the body should not remain there overnight, but should be buried on the same day, or the land would be defiled (see Deuteronomy 21:22-23). In the case of Jesus and the two criminals crucified alongside him the defilement would be worse, as the next day was a 'special Sabbath' (John 19:31, NIV) falling during Passover Week. The religious authorities had been viciously dishonest in hounding Jesus to death, yet they now insisted on maintaining ritual purity by observing this prohibition and asked Pilate for permission to remove the bodies for burial.

The usual way of making sure the victims were dead before taking them down was to have soldiers break their legs, when shock would have ended their lives. Pilate agreed to this, and soldiers broke the legs of the two criminals. Turning to Jesus, they 'saw that he was already dead' (John 19:33) but, to make certain, 'one of the soldiers pierced his

side with a spear, and at once there came out blood and water' (John 19:34). Immediately after death the blood in the chambers of the heart clots fairly quickly and then separates into plasma and red blood cells. A spear plunged into a person's side near the heart would have released these two fluids, which a layman like John might well describe as 'blood and water'. On the other hand, as well as enlarging the heart chambers with blood, the shocking trauma Jesus suffered during the scourging and crucifixion could have caused such a build-up of fluid in the pericardium, a sac of fibrous tissue surrounding the heart, that a spear piercing this soon after death and before the blood congealed would have produced a flow of 'blood and water'. Whatever the exact explanation, one thing is certain — what was left hanging on that middle cross was a blood-soaked corpse.

THE SPECTATORS

So far we have looked at what led to the crucifixion of Jesus and at the horrific event itself. To understand what really lay behind it we now need to take a much closer look at the victim. We can do this from several different angles, all recorded in the Bible.

There was nothing unusual about crucifixion at that time. The Jewish historian Josephus records that around 40 BC Publius Quinctilius Varus, the Roman governor of Syria, had 2,000 Jewish rebels crucified in a single day. Crucifixion was usually reserved for slaves, the worst of criminals, military deserters, traitors and rebels against the state.

To add to its humiliating nature, crucifixion was a public event, and three crucifixions due to take place at the same time would probably attract a fair-sized crowd. What did they make of Jesus?

For the members of the execution squad he was just another criminal, and putting him to death just another day's work. Once they were satisfied that they had nailed Jesus' naked body firmly to the cross, the four soldiers concerned each claimed one piece of his clothing. They then gambled to decide who should have the one remaining item (see John 19:23-24) before taunting him by shouting, 'If you are the King of the Jews, save yourself!' (Luke 23:36-37).

Many in the watching crowd were nothing more than idle onlookers, who had 'assembled for this spectacle' (Luke 23:48) and just 'stood by, watching' (Luke 23:35). For some, reports of his claims and miracles would ring hollow now that he seemed unable to resist the Roman and Jewish authorities. They 'derided him, wagging their heads and saying, "You who would destroy the temple and rebuild it in three days, save yourself! If you are the Son of God, come down from the cross"' (Matthew 27:39-40).

The religious leaders who had hounded Jesus to death joined in the mockery: 'He saved others; he cannot save himself. He is the King of Israel; let him come down now from the cross, and we will believe in him' (Matthew 27:42). The robbers who were crucified with him 'also reviled him in the same way' (Matthew 27:44).

Some had very different emotions. For Mary, Jesus' mother, standing by the cross (John 19:25), there was the terrible trauma of seeing what was being done to her firstborn son, while other family members and close friends would also have anguished over what was happening. Even without family ties, followers of Jesus (John is the only one of the twelve disciples specifically mentioned as being present) would have been devastated at seeing their dearest friend humiliated, tortured and put to death in this way.

Some onlookers may have been seeing Jesus for the first time and some may have come across him earlier that week, when he was 'teaching daily in the temple' (Luke 19:47). Yet for his closest followers their agony was mingled with memories of the previous three years spent in his company — and what memories they must have shared!

THE MEMORIES

When Jesus was twelve years old he had spent time in the temple during Passover Week, discussing religious issues with some of the nation's leading theologians. Not only was he 'listening to them and asking them questions' (Luke 2:46) — something to be expected from a young boy — but he was also addressing questions which they put to him, and 'all who heard him were amazed at his understanding *and his*

answers' (Luke 2:47, emphasis added). During his public ministry his disciples had the benefit of this amazing wisdom at first hand. They saw crowds 'astonished at his teaching, for he was teaching them as one who had authority,

Excavations on the site of the temple

and not as their scribes' (Matthew 7:28-29). When he taught in his local synagogue in Nazareth, those who heard him were 'astonished' and asked, 'Where did this man get his wisdom and these mighty works?' (Matthew 13:54). Officers sent to arrest him returned to their masters empty-handed, explaining that they dare not lay hands on him, as 'No one ever spoke like this man!' (John 7:46). *Why the cross* for someone whose teaching enlightened and revolutionized the thinking of count-less people?

Others would have remembered, or have heard, that 'he went about doing good' (Acts 10:38) and that when he saw people in need 'he had compassion on them' (Matthew 14:14). At one point 'a great multitude of people from all Judea and Jerusalem and the sea coast of Tyre and Sidon' flocked after him (Luke 6:17), yet, far from revelling in his popularity, he remained 'gentle and lowly in heart' (Matthew 11:29). He behaved no differently when attacked: 'When they hurled their insults at him, he did not retaliate; when he suffered, he made no threats' (1 Peter 2:23, NIV). Reflecting on this, the apostle Paul wrote of 'the meekness and gentleness of Christ' (2 Corinthians 10:1). Unlike those who were self-centred, Jesus 'did not please himself' (Romans 15:3) and constantly put the interests of others before his own. *Why the cross* for a man like this?

THE MIRACLES

Jesus' love and compassion were demonstrated in his astonishing miracles. At the beginning of his ministry we find him 'healing every disease and every affliction among the people' (Matthew 4:23). This does not mean that he left behind a trail of sickness-free zones, but he did heal countless people, including those suffering from blindness, deafness, organic disorders, paralysis and demon possession. Leprosy was considered incurable in those days, and sufferers from the disease were social outcasts, to be avoided at all costs. Yet when a man with leprosy asked him for help, Jesus reached out his hand and healed him with a touch (see Mark 1:40-45). On another occasion he healed ten lepers at once (see Luke 17:11-19). On at least three occasions he raised people from the dead — the young daughter of Jairus, who was a ruling synagogue elder (Matthew 9:18-19,23-26), a young man whose body was being carried to the local cemetery (Luke 7:11-17), and a personal friend called Lazarus who had been dead and buried for four days (John 11:1-44).

Nor were his miracles limited to physical healing. His first recorded miracle was turning water into wine at a wedding (see John 2:1-12). Faced with a hungry crowd of 5,000 people, he fed them all with five loaves and two fish (see Matthew 14:13-21). Later he fed 4,000 with seven loaves and a few small fish (see Mark 8:1-21). When his disciples were in danger of drowning in a violent storm on the Sea of Galilee he stilled the wind and the waves with a word (see Luke 8:22-25). There were also countless other miracles of which we have no written record. John's Gospel ends with the words: 'Now  there are also many other things that Jesus did. Were every one of them to be written, I suppose that the world itself could not contain the books that would be written' (John 21:25). It has been suggested that Jesus may have performed more miracles in one day than were performed in 1,000 years of Old Testament history. Be that as it may, his miracles demonstrated not only his power but his love, compassion and kindness. *Why the cross* for a man whose life was spent serving others in such miraculous ways?

THE TESTIMONIES

An even greater reason for seeing the crucifixion of Jesus as an appalling travesty of justice is the Bible's insistence that he was not merely a man of outstanding moral integrity, but that he was blameless in all he ever thought, said or did. We get hints of this in remarkable testimonies given just before his death. Pontius Pilate told the chief priests and crowds, 'I find no guilt in this man' (Luke 23:4). During the second trial, Pilate's wife urged him, 'Have nothing to do with that righteous man' (Matthew 27:19). When one of the criminals crucified at the same time called on Jesus to rescue them all, his partner in crime replied, 'Don't you fear God ... since you are under the same sentence? We are punished justly, for we are getting what our deeds deserve. But this man has done nothing wrong' (Luke 23:40-41, NIV). As Jesus drew his final breath, the centurion in charge of the execution squad declared, 'Surely this was a righteous man' (Luke 23:47, NIV).

These may be impressions gained over the course of just a few hours, but they point us in the right direction. Judas Iscariot's confession that he had sinned by betraying 'innocent blood' (Matthew 27:4) is much more impressive, as he had spent three years in Jesus' company and had every opportunity to see and hear him at close hand. This convinced him not only that Jesus should not be sentenced to death, but that he had no moral flaws.

Peter, a local fisherman and one of Jesus' first twelve disciples, had also spent over three years in Jesus' company and testified that his life had been 'without blemish' (1 Peter 1:19). As someone who at times had spoken rashly and deceitfully, he was well qualified to contrast his own behaviour with that of Jesus, who 'committed no sin, neither was deceit found in his mouth' (1 Peter 2:22). John, a disciple who had a particularly close relationship with Jesus, had no hesitation in calling him 'righteous' (1 John 2:29). This is the same word used by the Roman centurion at the cross, yet from John it carries much more weight. Another New Testament writer says that Jesus was 'holy, innocent, unstained, separated from sinners' (Hebrews 7:26) and that, although 'in every respect ... tempted as we are', he was 'without sin' (Hebrews 4:15).

The apostle Paul had once been on a personal crusade to destroy the Christian church and wipe out all Jesus' followers, yet the thinking of this brilliant, highly educated man was transformed. He had once considered Jesus a blasphemous deceiver whose teaching threatened the religious life of the entire nation, yet became convinced that Jesus 'knew no sin' (2 Corinthians 5:21). Paul was later to be flogged, tortured, imprisoned, stoned and 'exposed to death again and again' (2 Corinthians 11:23, NIV) for his beliefs, yet he never once flinched from his conviction that Jesus had no moral or spiritual flaws. *Why the cross* for someone whose words, actions, life and lifestyle had convinced so many people that he was faultless?

THE PROPHECIES

The Old Testament (the first part of the Bible) has thirty-nine books written by over twenty authors, some anonymous, but it is not a random collection of unrelated material. Instead, it has one unifying theme — God's dealings with mankind at large and with the Jewish nation in particular. Central to this was the promise that God would one day break into human history by sending a great deliverer to deal with humankind's greatest problem, its separation from God because of sin. This deliverer would eventually be known as 'the Messiah' (which means 'the anointed one'). Old Testament prophets, priests and kings were anointed with oil when they took office, symbolizing their authority to serve God, but none was called 'the Messiah'. Many prophets wrote about the coming Messiah, and the last of them brought this assurance from God: 'The messenger of the covenant, whom you desire, will come' (Malachi 3:1, NIV).

There were no further Messianic prophecies for 400 years — then Jesus came on the scene. Worshipping in his local synagogue in Nazareth when he was about thirty years old, he was handed a scroll containing part of the Old Testament and stood to read these words:

> The Spirit of the Lord is upon me,
> > because he has anointed me to proclaim good news to the poor.
> He has sent me to proclaim liberty to the captives
> > and recovering of sight to the blind,
> > to set at liberty those who are oppressed,
> to proclaim the year of the Lord's favour
>
> (Luke 4:18-19).

Those present would have heard these words many times, as they were part of a well-known passage written by the prophet Isaiah and promising the coming of the Messiah, but what happened next was electrifying. With 'the eyes of all in the synagogue … fixed on him', Jesus declared, 'Today this Scripture has been fulfilled in your hearing' (Luke 4:20,21).

The impact was stunning. Here was the son of a local tradesman claiming that Isaiah's prophecy was about him! The

Scroll of part of the Hebrew Old Testament

listeners' first impression was favourable, but as he developed the implications of his claim, they quickly turned against him and he narrowly escaped being thrown over a nearby cliff.

Over the next three years, Jesus continued to underline his amazing claim, regardless of any opposition. In doing so he quoted from twenty-four Old Testament books, drawing on all three major sections of the Old Testament, 'the Law of Moses and the Prophets and the Psalms' (Luke 24:44). To give one remarkable example, Daniel prophesied in the Old Testament that the coming Messiah would be 'one like a son of man' (Daniel 7:13) — and Jesus applied the title 'Son of Man' to himself nearly eighty times.

Sceptics may argue that this proves nothing, as history is littered with stories of people making outrageous or bizarre claims. A school student with a reputation for embarrassing guest speakers once challenged me by saying that when Jesus discovered he had been born in Bethlehem and in a family descended from Israel's King David (both of which had been prophesied in the Old Testament) he simply made sure that he fulfilled the other Messianic prophecies. In reply I pointed out that he would have needed to fulfil about 300 in all — and that arranging to be born of a virgin (prophesied in the Old Testament and recorded in the New Testament) would have presented more than a little difficulty! The sceptic never said another word.

Even if we begin with the Old Testament patriarch Abraham, who lived about 2,000 years before Jesus was born, we would see that the Messiah's family tree followed God's precisely-drawn line. God promised Abraham, 'In you all the families of the earth shall be blessed' (Genesis 12:3), which meant that the Messiah would come from Abraham's family. The line can then be traced through Abraham's son Isaac (not his other son Ishmael), then Isaac's son Jacob (not his other son Esau), then Jacob's fourth son, Judah (bypassing the other eleven). The same remarkable process went on for hundreds of years, always within Abraham's family line, until it reached Israel's King David.

The opening verse of Matthew's Gospel calls Jesus 'the son of David, the son of Abraham' (Matthew 1:1), but as he was not born until about thirty generations after David (Matthew traces these) the word 'son' obviously means 'descendant'. What Matthew makes clear is that Jesus ticked all the right boxes as far as the Messianic line of descent was concerned.

Even his place of birth was pinpointed precisely. God had promised:

But you, Bethlehem Ephrathah,
    though you are small among the clans of Judah,
out of you will come for me
    one who will be ruler over Israel

(Micah 5:2, NIV).

View of Bethlehem today

There were two Bethlehems, one in the region of Ephrathah in Judea, and the other in Zebulun, seventy miles to the north. The prophecy made it clear that the first of these would be the birthplace of the Messiah — and the New Testament tells us that 'Jesus was born in Bethlehem of Judea' (Matthew 2:1).

From then on, Jesus' life fulfilled hundreds of prophecies about the Messiah, covering his family's social status, his lifestyle, his character and his amazing powers. His miracles of healing alone fulfilled a Messianic prophecy made over 700 years earlier:

Then the eyes of the blind shall be opened,
    and the ears of the deaf unstopped;
then shall the lame man leap like a deer,
    and the tongue of the mute sing for joy

(Isaiah 35:5-6).

The picture becomes even clearer when we discover that nearly thirty Old Testament prophecies about the Messiah were fulfilled by Jesus in the twenty-four hours leading up to his death. Here are ten, with the New Testament record of their fulfilment:

• One of the psalmists has the Messiah saying, 'Even my close friend in whom I trusted, who ate my bread, has lifted his heel against me' (Psalm 41:9). Judas Iscariot, one of Jesus' inner circle of disciples, betrayed him to the religious authorities.
• The same psalmist prophesies, 'Malicious witnesses rise up' (Psalm 35:11). At Jesus' trial before Caiaphas 'many false witnesses came forward' (Matthew 26:60).
• Isaiah movingly records the Messiah saying:

I gave my back to those who strike,
    and my cheeks to those who pull out the beard;

I hid not my face
　　from disgrace and spitting

(Isaiah 50:6).

Matthew records that when the soldiers were humiliating the blindfolded Jesus, 'they spat in his face and struck him. And some slapped him, saying, "Prophesy to us, you Christ! Who is it that struck you?"' (Matthew 26:67-68).
• Isaiah writes:

He was oppressed, and he was afflicted,
　　yet he opened not his mouth;
like a lamb that is led to the slaughter,
　　and like a sheep that before its shearers is silent,
　　so he opened not his mouth

(Isaiah 53:7).

Pilate tried to browbeat Jesus into convicting himself. 'But he gave him no answer, not even to a single charge, so that the governor was greatly amazed' (Matthew 27:14).
• Isaiah also prophesies of the Messiah that he was to be 'numbered with the transgressors' (Isaiah 53:12). Matthew records of Jesus that 'two robbers were crucified with him, one on the right and one on the left' (Matthew 27:38).
• In one of his psalms, David has the Messiah crying:

All who see me mock me;
　　they hurl insults, shaking their heads:
'He trusts in the LORD;
　　let the LORD rescue him.
Let him deliver him,
　　since he delights in him'

(Psalm 22:7-8, NIV).

Matthew records the Jewish religious rulers mocking Jesus as he hung on the cross and crying, 'Let him come down now from the cross, and we will believe in him. He trusts in God; let God deliver him now, if he desires him' (Matthew 27:42-43).

• In another psalm, David prophesies, 'He keeps all his bones; not one of them is broken' (Psalm 34:20). After the three men had been crucified, soldiers came to ensure that they were dead by breaking their legs. 'But when they came to Jesus and saw that he was already dead, they did not break his legs' (John 19:33).

• Zechariah sees the Messiah crying, 'They look on me, on him whom they have pierced' (Zechariah 12:10). John tells us that to make sure Jesus was dead, a soldier 'pierced his side with a spear' (John 19:34).

• Jeremiah prophesies about actions involving elders, priests, the blood of the innocent, a potter's field and a burial place (see Jeremiah 19:1-15) and Zechariah prophesies about someone being valued at 'thirty pieces of silver' (Zechariah 11:13). Matthew records that after Judas Iscariot realized his appalling sin in betraying Jesus he threw the money into the temple, but that the priests and elders (calling it 'blood money') took it and used it to buy 'the potter's field as a burial place for strangers' (Matthew 27:6,7).

• David writes, 'They divide my garments among them, and for my clothing they cast lots' (Psalm 22:18). Matthew records that after they had crucified Jesus the Roman soldiers 'divided his garments among them by casting lots' (Matthew 27:35).

Surely this evidence is a powerful pointer to his identity? It is hardly surprising that in the New Testament Jesus is identified as 'Christ' (the Greek translation of the Old Testament 'Messiah') about 600 times. Suggestions that Jesus 'fixed' things to bolster his claim generate more heat than light, and for the British author and broadcaster Sir Ludovic Kennedy to dismiss all the Messianic prophecies as 'bogus' says more about him than it does about them. *Why the cross* for the one person in all history whose birth, life and death pointed to his being God's promised Messiah?

THE SON

Christianity is based on the identity of its founder rather than on his teaching, and Jesus' identity was constantly in the spotlight. When he went to Jerusalem, 'The whole city was stirred up, saying, "Who is

this?"' (Matthew 21:10). When he calmed a storm on the Sea of Galilee, his friends asked, 'Who then is this, that even wind and sea obey him?' (Mark 4:41). When he pardoned a re-pentant prostitute, people asked, 'Who is this, who even forgives sins?' (Luke 7:49). Baffled as to the true identity of Jesus, Herod asked, 'Who is this about whom I hear such things?' (Luke 9:9). Nothing is more important at this point than to find the right answer to that question.

The arrival of the Messiah was hugely significant for the Jewish nation, but the Bible identifies Jesus in two even more amazing ways, both with universal importance. The first comes in John's Gospel, which begins by describing Jesus as 'the only Son from the Father' (John 1:14) and ends by stating that 'Jesus is the Christ, the Son of God' (John 20:31). To say that Jesus is the Son of God does not mean that God the Father produced a son, as a human father does. This would make Jesus the Father's offspring, which is not the case. Within the Godhead, the Father and the Son had a relationship that went far beyond any that exists within a human family. Jesus underlined this when he told people, 'You are from below; I am from above' (John 8:23), and he made it even clearer by telling his disciples, 'No one knows the Father except the Son' (Matthew 11:27). Jesus is not merely *a* son of God, but *the* Son of God, 'the only Son from the Father' (John 1:14).

Jesus had a birth, but no beginning. His life did not begin at his conception, nor even at his birth, which merely marked his appearance on earth as a human being. Unlike all other human beings, *he chose to be born*, to add human nature to his divine nature, though without ever ceasing to be divine. There was a time when Jesus was not a man, but never a time when he was not God. He was eternally the Son of God; at a given point in time he chose to step into history, reveal himself as the Son of Man and combine two natures in one person. We can never understand this, but it is firmly embedded in the Bible.

Jesus pinned down this unique claim when Caiaphas the high priest asked him, 'I charge you under oath by the living God: Tell us if you are the Christ, the Son of God', by replying, 'Yes, it is as you say' (Matthew 26:63,64, NIV). *Why the cross* for the only person in history who demonstrated that his claim to be the Son of God was true?

THE LORD

For Jesus to be identified as the Son of God is amazing, but the Bible goes even further — it says *he was God*. Nor do we have to look for an obscure text that might be twisted to mean this. As C. S. Lewis wrote, 'The doctrine of Christ's divinity seems to me not something stuck on which you can unstick ... you would have to unravel the whole web to get rid of it.'[2] Jesus said that to believe in him was to believe in God (see John 12:44), to receive him was to receive God (see Mark 9:37), to honour him was to honour God (see John 5:23), to hate him was to hate God (see John 15:23), to know him was to know God (see John 8:19) and to see him was to see God (see John 14:9).

The deity of Jesus is underlined by the fact that the Bible gives him the title 'Lord'. Rather than risk blasphemy by using his sacred name (the Hebrew word *Yahweh*) lightly, Jews in Old Testament times created three special titles for God. In the first Greek translation of the Old Testament each of these was translated *kyrios*, which became the most commonly used word for God. Yet the apostle Paul uses *kyrios* about 200 times to refer to Jesus, calling the title 'the name that is above every name' (see Philippians 2:9-11). The Bible is crystal clear —'Jesus is Lord [*kyrios*]' (Romans 10:9) — and, as a biblical scholar has said, to declare these words is to acknowledge that Jesus 'shares the name and the nature, the holiness, the authority, power, majesty and eternity of the one and only true God'.[3]

Looking for a visible appearance of God to reinforce their faith, one of Jesus' disciples asked him, 'Lord, show us the Father, and it is enough for us' (John 14:8). Jesus replied, 'Have I been with you so long, and you still do not know me, Philip? Whoever has seen me has seen the Father' (John 14:9). He was not claiming to *be* the Father, but to be the visible manifestation of God, revealing all of God's character and nature that it was possible and necessary for anyone to see and know. In other words, he was claiming to be God.

I have written more fully about this elsewhere,[4] but here are some of the ways in which the Bible confirms the deity of Jesus Christ. It says, 'For by him all things were created, in heaven and on earth, visible and invisible' (Colossians 1:16); *this can be said only of God.* It says that 'he upholds the universe by the word of his

power' (Hebrews 1:3); *this can be said only of God*. It says that at the end
of time he will 'judge the living and the dead' (2 Timothy 4:1); *this can
be said only of God*. The Bible could not be clearer: 'He is the radiance of
the glory of God and the exact imprint of his nature' (Hebrews 1:3); 'In
him the whole fullness of deity dwells bodily' (Colossians 2:9).

Some people accept that Jesus was a great teacher, a man of outstanding wisdom, or someone who set a unique moral example, yet
refuse to accept that he was God in human form. C. S. Lewis easily
shows that this will not do:

> That is the one thing we must not say. A man who was merely
> a man and said the sort of things Jesus said would not be a great
> moral teacher. He would either be a lunatic — on a level with the
> man who says he is a poached egg — or else he would be the
> devil of hell. You must make your choice... You can shut him up
> for a fool; you can spit at him and kill him as a demon; or you can
> fall at his feet and call him Lord and God. But let us not come up
> with any patronizing nonsense about his being a great human
> teacher. He has not left that open to us. He did not intend to.[5]

Why the cross for the man who was God?

THE HUMBLING

Our close look at the victim ought to convince us that the crucifixion of
Jesus should never have taken place. Not only was he innocent of every
charge brought against him, but he was without fault of any kind. Now
we need to dig even deeper, because the Bible makes it clear that in
order to grasp the meaning of his death we need to go back to his birth
— and beyond that. This will explain what really happened on the cross
and why Jesus chose to go through with it. The Bible takes us there
with this stupendous statement:

… though he was in the form of God, [he] did not count equality with God a thing to be grasped, but made himself nothing, taking the form of a servant, being born in the likeness of men. And being found in human form, he humbled himself by becoming obedient to the point of death, even death on a cross (Philippians 2:6-8).

In these two sentences there are eight great truths; we dare not miss one of them.

- Jesus was *'in the form of God'*. This does not mean that he had the same size or shape as God, as 'God is spirit' (John 4:24) and has neither of these. It means that *even before time began* Jesus had all of God's attributes and nature. To put it simply, he was eternally, truly and totally God.
- He *'did not count equality with God a thing to be grasped'*. Glorious as his heavenly existence was, he did not cling to it as if nothing else mattered, but relinquished it in the interests of others.
- He *'made himself nothing'*. The phrase literally means 'he emptied himself', underlining what we have just seen. He laid aside the majesty and glory that were eternally his in heaven — though without giving up any of his divine nature.
- He *'[took] the form of a servant'*. Just as he was truly God, so he truly became a servant, not only of his heavenly Father, but also of mankind. As he himself told his followers, 'I am among you as the one who serves' (Luke 22:27).
- He was *'born in the likeness of men'*. He became what he had never been before. He remained fully divine, yet became fully human. As the British theologian J. I. Packer writes:

God became man; the divine Son became a Jew; the Almighty appeared on earth as a helpless human baby, unable to do more than stare and wriggle and make noises, needing to be fed and changed and taught like any other child... The more you think about it, the more staggering it gets.[6]

• He was *'found in human form'*. Although his outward appearance was normal (he did not have a halo or wings), there was more to him than met the eye. Those who called him 'the carpenter's son' (Matthew 13:55) missed a far greater truth. Although he remained divine, he was a real man, not merely disguised as one.

• He *'humbled himself'*. In leaving heaven for earth Jesus was not a conscript but a volunteer. He *chose* to leave eternity and submit himself to the limitations of time and space.

• He became *'obedient to the point of death, even death on a cross'*. He knew exactly what would be involved in his earthly mission. He was not trapped in a Catch-22 situation and forced into something against his will. Though he would need to die to accomplish his life's mission, he never flinched from paying that price. Death on a cross was a barbaric form of execution, not practised by his own people, the Jews, and reserved by the Romans for those they considered the scum of society.

Then why did God, in the person of Jesus Christ, leave heaven, become a human being, submit to all the hardships and pressures of life on earth, and allow himself to be reviled, persecuted, tortured and eventually put to death in the most degrading way known to man? The answer is summed up in something the apostle Paul wrote to a group of early Christians at Corinth:

For you know the grace of our Lord Jesus Christ, that though he was rich, yet for your sake he became poor, so that you by his poverty might become rich (2 Corinthians 8:9).

Examining this statement phrase by phrase will give us the answer we need.

THE RICHES

To say of Jesus that *'he was rich'* before he was born may be the greatest understatement of all time, as his riches were far beyond our understanding.

He was rich in possessions

The Bible tells us, 'For by him all things were created, in heaven and on earth, visible and invisible, whether thrones or dominions or rulers or authorities — all things were *created through him and for him'* (Colossians 1:16, emphasis added). Every created thing, from the vastest galaxy to the tiniest particle in the universe, owes its existence to him. There is not an atom, a molecule, a neutron, a proton, a photon, an electron, a quasar or a quark which is not his by right of creation. As the Dutch theologian Abraham Kuyper put it, 'There is not a square inch in the whole domain of our human existence over which Christ, who is Sovereign over *all*, does not cry: "Mine!" '[7]

He was rich in authority

Centuries before Jesus was born Isaiah prophesied:

> Of the increase of his government and of peace
>   there will be no end,
> on the throne of David and over his kingdom,
>   to establish it and to uphold it
> with justice and with righteousness,
>   from this time forth and for evermore
>
>   (Isaiah 9:7).

Another prophecy acknowledged him as a king whose throne is 'as the days of the heavens' (Psalm 89:29), while in the New Testament we read of 'angels, authorities, and powers' being 'subjected to him' (1 Peter 3:22).

He was rich in power

The universe is not a haphazard collection of unrelated objects, but is governed by natural laws that give it order and integrity. The Bible tells us that these laws are determined and maintained by Jesus Christ, the one in whom 'all things hold together' (Colossians 1:17). It is *his* awesome power that prevents the cosmos from disintegrating into chaos. As the modern French author Guy Appéré puts it, 'It is impossible to explain either the future or the past, the end or the beginning of the universe ... apart from Jesus Christ.'[8]

He was rich in honour

In the last book of the Bible we find every living creature worshipping Jesus and ascribing to him 'blessing and honour and glory and might for ever and ever' (Revelation 5:13). If all the honours and awards, tributes and trophies, decorations and distinctions given in human history could be valued, they would be like cheap costume jewellery compared to the infinite honour eternally due to Jesus.

He was rich in glory

Praying to God the Father, Jesus spoke of 'the glory that I had with you before the world existed' (John 17:5). Again, we are out of our depth. Our minds are incapable of grasping the splendour of God's glory, which is so wonderful that even the highest angelic beings cover their faces in his presence (see Isaiah 6:2).

THE POVERTY

We are then told that Jesus *'became poor'*, another massive understatement beyond our reach. When he added human nature to his divine nature this brought poverty, something he had never known before. He exchanged the perfect harmony of heaven for the turmoil of life on earth, with its pressures and pains, trials and tensions, conflicts and crises. He exchanged being worshipped by angels for being reviled by his enemies. The one by whom 'all things were created' (Colossians 1:16) had to borrow a boat to cross the Sea of Galilee (see Mark 4:35-41), a donkey to ride into Jerusalem (see Luke 19:28-40) and a coin to give an illustration (see Luke 20:19-26). The one who owned every square inch of Earth was so poor that he had 'nowhere to lay his head' (Luke 9:58). The one who created water as a liquid compound with its molecule made up of one oxygen atom and two hydrogen atoms (H_2O) had to ask someone to give him a drink when he became thirsty (see John 4:1-7). Even in death his corpse was laid in a borrowed tomb (Matthew 27:57-61).

These are vivid illustrations of what it meant for the one who created all time, space and matter to step into their limitations. It was a humiliation without parallel. To raise awareness of the city's homeless problem, Britain's Prince William once opted to spend the night in an old sleeping bag on a 'mattress' of cardboard boxes in an alleyway near Blackfriars Bridge,

Blackfriars Bridge at night

London. The overnight temperature fell to -4°C and a spokesman said
that the prince may have only had 'a couple of hours' sleep'. Yet the
spot was carefully chosen for safety, the prince was accompanied by an
armed personal protection officer, his private secretary and the chief
executive of Centrepoint, the charity of which he was patron — and, as
the *Daily Mail* commented, 'He did have the prospect of a big lunch at
Buckingham Palace the next day to keep his spirits up.'[9] His gesture
was highly commendable, but it does not bear any resemblance to what
Jesus did in becoming a man.

C. S. Lewis once wrote, 'The Eternal Being who knows everything
and who created the whole universe became not only a man but (before
that) a baby, and before that a [foetus] inside a woman's body. If you
want to get the hang of it, think how you would like to become a slug
or a crab.'[10] Yet even this gets nowhere near the staggering truth of
what happened when Jesus laid aside his heavenly glory and chose to
become human, a truth made even more amazing when we read that he
did this *'for your sake'*. Jesus had nothing to gain from humbling himself,
restricting himself to time and space, exposing himself to trauma and
temptation and allowing himself to be mocked and rejected, tortured
and crucified. Instead, he did all this *for others*.

THE BIG WORDS

We are then told that Jesus' aim was *'so that you by his poverty might
become rich'*. Seven major words that Christians use to summarize the
Bible's teaching on what happened when Jesus died will help us to
understand how desperately poor we are by nature and how rich we
can become by 'the grace of our Lord Jesus Christ'.

Substitution

The basic meaning of the word is very straightforward and in relation to
the death of Jesus is extremely important. This comes across powerfully

when we read that 'Christ died for sins once for all, *the righteous for the unrighteous*, to bring you to God' (1 Peter 3:18, NIV, emphasis added). As another New Testament writer puts it, 'He laid down his life *for us*' (1 John 3:16, emphasis added). The Bible tells us that death is the result of sin; so how could Jesus die when he did not have a sinful nature and never committed sin of any kind? The Bible's answer is that in his death Jesus was bearing sin's penalty (which he did not deserve) in the place of others (who did). His death was certainly an impressive example of meekness, forgiveness and faith, but it was much more than that. Neither setting the finest example nor following it can make sinners right with God. As the British preacher John Stott says, 'A pattern cannot secure our pardon.'[11] Jesus was more than an example; he was a *substitute*, taking the place of those whose sin leaves them spiritually bankrupt and exposed to God's righteous anger. In the most amazing act of love ever known, Jesus endured sin's ultimate penalty in the place of even the worst of his enemies.

Propitiation

This is not an everyday word, but it is vitally important that we understand it. 'Propitiation' means appeasing an offended person by paying the penalty he demands for the offence. This enables him to receive back into his favour the person who committed the offence. In the New Testament the original Greek word for 'propitiation' is sometimes translated 'atonement'. This is easier to understand, as to 'atone' means to deal with an offence so that the offender and the person offended can be 'at one'. This is what Jesus did in dying on behalf of others: 'In this is love, not that we have loved God but that he loved us and sent his Son to be the propitiation for our sins' (1 John 4:10).

Many people think of God only as a God of love, always on hand to help when things go wrong and bound in the end to forgive everybody's sins and receive them into heaven for ever. This idea is fatally misleading. The Bible certainly tells us that 'God is love' (1 John 4:8), but also that he is 'majestic in holiness' (Exodus 15:11) and that 'the wrath of God is revealed from heaven against all ungodliness and unrighteousness of men' (Romans 1:18). A few years ago it was all the rage for some Christians to wear a badge saying, 'Smile, God loves you', but, as a friend of mine said at the time, 'It would be more truthful to wear one saying, "Frown, you're under judgement."'

Jesus showed the cost of being the propitiation for sin when on the cross he cried out, 'My God, my God, why have you forsaken me?' (Matthew 27:46). Only hours before, when his closest friends were about to desert him, he had assured them, 'I am not alone, for the Father is with me' (John 16:32). Yet in his dying moments that assurance was gone. Why? Christians often have a joyful sense of God's presence as they die, yet for Jesus exactly the opposite was true because at that moment he was experiencing not merely physical death but *spiritual* death. As the Bible puts it, 'God made him who had no sin *to be sin for us*, so that in him we might become the righteousness of God' (2 Corinthians 5:21, NIV, emphasis added). God has 'zero tolerance' of sin, and his holiness demands that all sin be punished. When Jesus became accountable for the sins of others he was punished as though he had committed them, and he bore that punishment both in his body and in his soul. When Jesus cried that he had been forsaken by God the Father, it did not mean that the Father was not there (as God is always everywhere), but that *he was not there to strengthen, comfort and bless him*. Instead, in his righteous anger against sin, God the Father deserted, rejected and punished him. As the American theologian R. C. Sproul puts it, at that moment the figure of Jesus on the cross 'was the most grotesque, most obscene mass of concentrated sin in the history of the world'. [12]

Ransom

This is a very familiar word. We all know of people taken prisoner by someone who then demands a ransom. The Bible teaches that sin not only separates sinners from God but imprisons them. They are 'slaves of sin' (Romans 6:17). What is more, sinners are not merely the captives of a sinful principle, but they are in 'the snare of the devil, after being captured by him to do his will' (2 Timothy 2:26). Most people reject this, but every sinful habit confirms its truth. Jesus said that he had come to 'give his life as a ransom for many' (Mark 10:45). His death on the cross was the essential ransom price so that God's justice could be satisfied and the sinners in whose place Jesus died set free.

Redemption

When a ransom has been paid, the captives are set free, or redeemed, and this is what happens to those for whom Jesus gave his life. The apostle Paul says that Jesus 'redeemed us from the curse of the law by becoming a curse for us' (Galatians 3:13). By nature we are under the 'curse' of God's holy law, which pronounces us guilty in his sight. Jesus was under no such curse, yet in order to satisfy the demands of divine justice he bore the curse of the law in full. The ransom price to bring redemption to helpless sinners was nothing less than his death in their place, and he paid it in full, setting prisoners of sin free to live in a way that is pleasing to God.

Forgiveness

The Bible sees sin as a debt owed by the sinner to God, but those on whose behalf Jesus died receive not only 'redemption through his blood' but also 'the forgiveness of sins' (Ephesians 1:7, NIV). In the death of Jesus the Christian believer is cut loose from the double burden of guilt and debt and is freely and fully forgiven — for ever.

Reconciliation

Reconciliation means bringing together those who are separated for one reason or another. By nature and choice we are all separated from God

because of our self-centred rebellion against his authority and our
determination to go our own way. As Jesus put it, 'The light has come
into the world, and people loved the darkness rather than the light
because their deeds were evil' (John 3:19). The Bible also says that
because of sin God has become man's enemy: 'For the wrath of God is
revealed from heaven against all ungodliness and unrighteousness of
men' (Romans 1:18).

Yet God (the innocent party) has taken the initiative and done
something astonishing to enable man (the guilty party) to be at peace
with him by dealing with the root cause of the rift — human sin. In the
death of his Son, God not only punished human sin but also satisfied
his own righteous judgement, and in this he way removed the barrier
separating him from sinners. This is why the apostle Paul writes, 'While
we were enemies we were reconciled to God by the death of his Son'
(Romans 5:10) and tells early Christians, 'You who once were far off
have been brought near by the blood of Christ' (Ephesians 2:13).

At the precise moment Jesus died, God provided an amazing visual
aid to illustrate this. In the temple in Jerusalem, the focal point of the
nation's worship, a richly-embroidered veil or curtain separated the
'Holy Place' from the 'Most Holy Place', the inner sanctuary that
represented God's presence. As Jesus drew his last breath, 'The curtain
of the temple was torn in two, from top to bottom' (Matthew 27:51).
This miracle was a sign that, whereas under the old religious system the
high priest alone could enter the symbolic presence of God, and then
only once a year, the death of Jesus had removed the sin barrier between God and man. Now, all those for whom he died could be reconciled to God without any religious trappings. Later, a first-century
Christian wrote, 'We have confidence to enter the Most Holy Place by
the blood of Jesus, by a new and living way opened for us through the
curtain, that is, his body' (Hebrews 10:19, NIV).

Justification

This word comes from the law courts. It describes what happens when a judge declares that the prisoner before him is not liable to any penalty demanded by the law and is to be treated as though he had never broken it. Yet, as sinners stand condemned by a God whose eyes are 'too pure to look on evil' and who 'cannot tolerate wrong' (Habakkuk 1:13, NIV), how can we possibly be declared 'Not Guilty' in his sight and treated as though we had never sinned? Jesus provides the answer. His perfect life met all the demands of God's law — he was 'holy, innocent, unstained, separated from sinners' (Hebrews 7:26) — and his death paid in full the penalty that God's law demands. Jesus was punished as though he had never been holy, so that those in whose place he died could be treated as though they had never been unholy. God declares a person righteous on the basis of the life and death of his Son, who was acting on that person's behalf. This is why the apostle Paul claims, 'Therefore, since we have been justified by faith, we have peace with God through our Lord Jesus Christ' (Romans 5:1). The justified sinner is brought into God's favour and family and received as though he had met all the demands of God's holy law. To be justified means to be made right with God for time and eternity.

What is more, the justified sinner receives eternal life *immediately*. When one of the criminals crucified alongside Jesus turned to him in faith, Jesus promised him, 'Truly, I say to you, *today* you will be with me in Paradise' (Luke 23:43, emphasis added). Their bodies would soon be buried, but the spirits of the sinner and his Saviour would by then be in heaven.

Left to ourselves, how poor are we? We are exposed to God's righteous anger, spiritually dead, prisoners of Satan and sin, helpless captives, hopelessly in debt to God, sworn enemies of our Creator and guilty without excuse or escape. How rich can we become because of Jesus' death? We can escape sin's death penalty, find favour with God, be set free from prison, escape from our self-imposed captivity, have all our sins forgiven, have spiritual peace and be right with God for ever.

THE PROOF

The 'big words' have revealed the most amazing promises, but how can we know that they are true and relevant to us today? The answer lies in the earth-shattering truth that *on the third day after he died and was buried Jesus rose from the dead!* A cross with a human body hanging on it completely misrepresents the Christian message. The symbol of Christianity is an *empty* cross, because the Bible's glorious message is that Jesus is alive today, having triumphed gloriously over sin and death. As C. S. Lewis put it:

> [Jesus] has forced open a door that has been locked since the death of the first man. He has met, fought and beaten the King of Death. Everything is different because he has done so. This is the beginning of the New Creation; a new chapter in cosmic history has opened.[13]

I have laid out the evidence for this stupendous truth elsewhere.[14] Here are some of the obvious pointers:

- Jesus undoubtedly died on the cross. Theories that he was buried while still alive and somehow recovered full health and strength again are absurd.
- Not even his worst enemies denied that by Sunday morning (Jesus died and was buried on Friday) his tomb was empty.
- If for some strange reason the Roman or Jewish authorities had removed the body from the tomb, they would have produced it as soon as Jesus' followers claimed that he was alive again and the Christian church would have collapsed on the spot.

A first-century garden tomb in Jerusalem

• As there was an armed guard of Roman soldiers at the tomb, Jesus' followers could not have stolen the body — nor would they have wanted to as it was buried safely in a friend's grave.

• Before Jesus rose from the dead his followers hid behind locked doors 'for fear of the Jews' (John 20:19). Yet a few weeks later they risked persecution, imprisonment, torture and even death because they had seen Jesus alive again. People sometimes die for something they believe to be true (even if it can be shown that it is not), *but nobody is prepared to die for something they know to be false,* especially if they concocted the lie.

• Six independent witnesses record Jesus appearing after his death in eleven separate incidents over a period of forty days. On one occasion over 500 saw him at the same time, and when the apostle Paul recorded this well over half of them were still alive and could confirm the fact (see 1 Corinthians 15:6).

• The Christian church is the largest religious body the world has ever known (over two billion and growing by the thousand every day) and no other group, religious or otherwise, has made a greater contribution to the well-being of humankind. Yet the church is not based on the moral example Jesus set, nor on his death, but on his resurrection. For 2,000 years this has been its driving force and *the only explanation for its existence.* The first Christian church was known as 'the Way' (Acts 9:2), but if Jesus had remained in the grave 'the Way' would have become a dead end! As the American preacher D. James Kennedy put it, 'The Grand Canyon wasn't caused by an Indian dragging a stick, and the Christian church wasn't created by a myth.'[15]

The Grand Canyon

THE MEANING

The Bible has 'many convincing proofs' (Acts 1:3, NIV) of the resurrection of Jesus — but what does it mean?

The Bible's first answer is that Jesus 'was declared to be the Son of God in power ... by his resurrection from the dead' (Romans 1:4). His resurrection did not *make* Jesus the Son of God, as he has always been so; it *proved* that he was. *It was a declaration of his deity.* It showed him to be everything he claimed to be. Before Jesus died his deity had been 'veiled' by his humanity, so that, in spite of his character, his teaching and his miracles, he was in many ways no different from others. His resurrection changed everything, and his divine power over death proved that he was exactly who he claimed to be. When he invited a disciple (ever since known as 'Doubting Thomas') to examine the wounds caused by his crucifixion so as to confirm that he had indeed risen, Thomas was convinced and cried out, 'My Lord and my God!' (John 20:28).

Yet his resurrection also proved that *his death was not a defeat but a glorious victory.* About a year before his death three of his disciples were given a glimpse of his divine glory and Jesus 'spoke of his departure, which he was about to accomplish at Jerusalem' (see Luke 9:28-36). Nobody speaks of 'accomplishing' their death, but Jesus did. His death did not conclude his life; it crowned it. Although he was crucified 'by the hands of lawless men', his death was 'according to the definite plan and foreknowledge of God' (Acts 2:23). Far from being something over which God had no control, or a knee-jerk reaction to an unforeseen crisis, it was something he had planned 'before the foundation of the world' (1 Peter 1:20).

This explains why, as he was dying, Jesus cried out, 'It is finished' (John 19:30). This was not a terrified cry of defeat, but a triumphant cry of victory. It meant 'mission accomplished', not 'mission abandoned'. Immediately prior to his arrest and execution he told his disciples, 'The hour has come for the Son of Man to be glorified,' and went on to say, 'for this purpose I have come to this hour' (John 12:23,27). In his death he achieved exactly what God the Father had sent him into the world to do (see John 17:4). Death did not annihilate him; it glorified him in what it achieved.

But how can we be sure of this? How do we know the price Jesus paid was accepted and the debt paid? Many years ago in Britain there were 'debtors' prisons', where those who could not pay what they owed were held under arrest. If someone had agreed to stand as a guarantor for the debtor and the debtor could not be found, the guarantor could be jailed in his place. If you had been the debtor and had left the country owing a large sum of money, your guarantor would have been jailed until the debt was cleared. If you returned and saw your guarantor walking the street as a free man you would know that the debt you had incurred had been paid in full on your behalf.

The illustration is not perfect, but the main point is clear. Jesus was 'imprisoned' by death on behalf of those in whose place he was acting, but when he had paid sin's penalty in full, 'God raised him from the dead, freeing him from the agony of death, because it was impossible for death to keep its hold on him' (Acts 2:24, NIV). The one who paid the debt was released from the prison of death. In the original language used, Jesus' last cry, 'It is finished', is just one word — *tetelestai* — a word that was often written across a bill when it had been paid in full. His resurrection is all the proof we need that those in whose place he died can never be asked to pay sin's debt again. As the twentieth-century American theologian Donald Grey Barnhouse put it, 'The resurrection of Christ is our receipted bill.' The person in whose place Jesus died can never be asked to pay the bill again.

THE INVITATION

For some forty years I have lived within fifteen miles of Buckingham Palace, the official residence of Queen Elizabeth II, the United Kingdom's head of state. I have been to Buckingham Palace once as a tourist,

Buckingham Palace

but never at Her Majesty's invitation. If I were to receive a royal invitation I would not treat it like any other, which I might choose to turn down. An invitation I received from my queen would to me be a command, and one I would feel under a willing obligation to obey. The same is true of an infinitely more important invitation, one that comes to everybody from the Lord Jesus Christ, who is 'the King of kings and Lord of lords' (1 Timothy 6:15). Let me spell it out as you come towards the end of this booklet.

Firstly, it is a genuine and loving invitation. To those concerned about their need to get right with God, but struggling under a mountain of rules and regulations imposed by the religious authorities, Jesus said, 'Come to me, all you who are weary and burdened, and I will give you rest' (Matthew 11:28, NIV). *He gives the same invitation today.* Religious observance can never make you right with God. Services and sacraments, rites and rituals can never bridge the gap that sin has created. But if you turn to Jesus and trust him to save you, he will release you from the burden of trying to get right with God by your own efforts and give you the 'rest' you need.

To those who found life empty, without meaning or purpose, Jesus said, 'I am the bread of life; whoever comes to me shall not hunger, and whoever believes in me shall never thirst' (John 6:35). *He issues the same invitation today.* He alone can give you spiritual life and then sustain you day by day as you seek to live for him.

To those who were concerned about their eternal destiny, Jesus said, 'Whoever hears my word and believes him who sent me has eternal life. He does not come into judgement, but has passed from death to life' (John 5:24). *He makes the same invitation today.* All who respond to it are promised that they will spend eternity in God's glorious presence in heaven, where there will be no more trials or traumas, fear or failure, sin or suffering, disease, decay or death.

These are amazing invitations and promises. Sinners are offered forgiveness; rebels are offered amnesty; enemies are offered friendship; outsiders are offered places in God's family; slaves to sin are offered release from its grip; prisoners are offered liberty; those doomed to spend eternity in hell are promised eternity in heaven — and all these are lovingly made to everybody, even those who deny God's existence or flatly reject the Bible's testimony that Jesus is divine.

Yet they are also commands. When Jesus said, 'Come to me', it was not a casual suggestion or a vague 'take it or leave it' offer, but a serious and firm instruction. Elsewhere God makes the wonderful promise, 'You will seek me and find me when you seek me with all your heart' (Jeremiah 29:13, NIV), but he also says, 'Seek the LORD while he may be found; call upon him while he is near' (Isaiah 55:6). This is a command, and to disobey it is outright rebellion.

You may receive many invitations of one kind of another. Some can be thrown away immediately, while deciding what to do about others is just a matter of choice, with no serious consequences. God's invitations and commands are very different, because left to yourself you are in clear and present danger. Not only are you helplessly exposed to God's righteous anger day after day (even if you are not aware of this), but by rejecting his invitation, made at such unimaginable cost, you are 'storing up [God's] wrath' for the day when 'God's righteous judgement will be revealed' (Romans 2:5). Some years ago I was in Greece at the time of a general election. On Election Day I was told that the polling booths opened at sunrise. When I asked, 'When do they close?' my host replied,

'The moment the sun sets.' I have never forgotten that. It is a powerful picture of the urgent need to respond to God's invitation to turn to him while you can. The opportunity to do so lasts only for as long as the 'sun' of one's life is in the sky — and nobody knows when it will set. God may not allow you another day, let alone another week, month or year, in which to turn to him. As the Bible warns you, 'Do not boast about tomorrow, for you do not know what a day may bring' (Proverbs 27:1). Whatever your age or state of health, at this moment you are twenty-four hours nearer your death than you were at this time yesterday. This is not being miserable or morbid; it is a simple fact. It is only by God's grace that you are being given the present opportunity to respond to his invitation, obey his command and lay hold on the promises of the forgiveness of sins and eternal life that he is making to you at this very moment. God says, 'I have no pleasure in the death of the wicked, but that the wicked turn from his way and live; turn back, turn back from your evil ways, for why will you die…?' (Ezekiel 33:11). *He says the same to you at this very moment.*

Are you ready to meet your Maker? Are you certain that you are right with God? Are you sure that your sins are forgiven and that when your life on earth ends you will spend eternity in heaven? If not, *call upon him now*, asking him to have mercy on you and to enable you to lay hold on the promises of the gospel. As you do, you will truly understand the answer to the question, 'Why the cross?'

NOTES

1. *The Observer*, 26 March 1967.
2. C. S. Lewis, *They Stand Together; The Letters of C. S. Lewis to Arthur Greeves*, Collins, p.503.
3. C. E. Cranfield, *A Critical and Exegetical Commentary on the Epistle to the Romans*, Continuum International Publishing Group, p.529.
4. John Blanchard, *Meet the real Jesus*, EP Books.
5. C. S. Lewis, *Mere Christianity*, Macmillan, p.52.
6. J. I. Packer, *Knowing God*, Hodder & Stoughton, p.53.
7. Abraham Kuyper, 'Sphere Sovereignty', in *Abraham Kuyper: A Centennial reader*, ed. James D. Bratt, Eerdmans, p.488.
8. Guy Appéré, *The Mystery of Christ*, Evangelical Press, p.43.
9. *Daily Mail*, 16 December 2009.
10. Lewis, *Mere Christianity*, p.152.
11. John R. W. Stott, *Basic Christianity*, Inter-Varsity Press, p.92.
12. R. C. Sproul, *The Truth of the Cross*, Reformation Trust, p.134.
13. C. S. Lewis, *Miracles*, Collins, p.149.
14. John Blanchard, *JESUS: Dead or Alive?*, EP Books.
15. D. James Kennedy, *The Gates of Hell Shall Not Prevail*, Thomas Nelson Publishers, p.21.